Spellbound Science

Book 1

By
Brenda Keogh and Stuart Naylor
Illustrations Laura Murray

Acknowledgments

The following team of people have made this publication possible.
Our thanks are due to all of them for their creative ideas.

LAURA MURRAY
Illustrator
KATHRYN STAWPERT
Graphic Design

DAVID OSBORN
and
MELISSA WOOD
at Angel Solutions
software development

CHILDREN
at Sandbach Primary School,
Cheshire and TEACHERS there and
elsewhere, helping to develop the
stories and characters

BRIGID DOWNING, JANE MALONEY,
SHIRLEY SIMON and the
PUPPET PROJECT TEACHERS
exploring with us the potential of
puppets in science

JOHN DABELL
Narration
and
THE ROOFTOP GROUP
Sound engineering

LAUREN BARNES
Project manager

KAY ROBERTS and FRANK ELLIS
at GlaxoSmithKline plc, their belief in our work will enable our puppet
characters, Ricky and Nana, and their stories to engage children in
stimulating scientific experiences

And finally
RICKY, RUBY, NANA, JED and LITTLE WIZARD,
whose ideas about science inspired us to create these stories.

Contents

Introduction

Welcome to Spellbound Science Book 1.

In this book you can read stories about Ricky and Nana's science problems. Ruby, Jed and Little Wizard all try to help them.

NOTE

When you see this icon you **MUST** get an **ADULT'S** help.

CHECK WITH AN ADULT

Hello I'm Ricky. Nana and I never seem to agree with each other. Can you help us to sort out our arguments?

Hello I'm Nana. We like to talk about our ideas. Why don't you do that too? See who you think is right. I think it might be me.

Brenda Keogh and Stuart Naylor 2007

Too Many Teeth

"Look at this, Ricky! It's so sharp!" Nana pointed to a tiger's tooth. "And look at this! It's gigantic!" She pointed to a hippopotamus's tooth. Nana and Ricky were visiting a dental laboratory. The laboratory made false teeth for animals that had lost their own teeth - cats' teeth, dogs' teeth, cows' teeth, tigers' teeth.

Ricky stared in amazement at the huge rack covered with dozens of teeth. He'd never seen anything like it. Every kind of tooth you could imagine. All the teeth were neatly labelled and lined up in tidy rows. His favourite ones were right at the very top of the rack. No one was looking, so he stretched up high to try to reach them.

Meanwhile, Nana had found a set of teeth that looked just like Grandad's. She was feeling very pleased that she had always looked after her teeth. Suddenly Nana heard an enormous CRASH. "What's that? What's happened?"

Ricky was standing still. He was surrounded by teeth - big teeth, little teeth, pointy teeth, curved teeth, straight teeth. The teeth were everywhere. They were all jumbled up. "Oh no!" Ricky said, looking horrified, "What will we do? We'll never get them back in the right order."

"Perhaps Little Wizard could help us," said Nana. She had hardly finished talking when, swoosh, there was Little Wizard standing in the middle of all the muddled teeth.

"Don't panic Ricky," said Little Wizard, waving his wand. "I can do a spell to sort out the teeth. There's only one problem. I'm not sure what kind of teeth each animal has. What size are they? And what shape?"

"Oops! Now that could be a problem," said Nana. "What if we get the teeth mixed up? What if a mouse gets cows' teeth, and a rabbit gets tigers' teeth?" Nana laughed at the thought of the different animals with all the wrong teeth.

"Don't laugh Nana, this isn't funny. What are we going to do?" Ricky asked.

At that point Ruby and Jed arrived. They were shocked to see teeth all over the floor. Ricky told them what had happened and how they needed to decide which were the right teeth for the different animals. They began to think about the problem and to talk about their ideas.

Try to think of your own ideas for finding out.
Here are some of our ideas for what you could do...

You could explore what the different teeth do. Can you find things that work like:

◎ flat molar teeth? e.g. nutcracker

◎ pointed canine teeth? e.g. a fork

◎ sharp incisor teeth? e.g. a pair of scissors

You could produce a set of information cards for different animals' teeth.

Each card could show...

❯ the animal
❯ what it eats
❯ how its teeth help it to eat that kind of food.

RABBIT

Eats   Plants

Two pairs of upper ....

Find out about the kinds of teeth that different animals have. You could:

◎ look in books or CDs

◎ do an internet image search

◎ look at the skulls and teeth of different animals in a museum.

Find out what you should do to keep your teeth healthy.

Are there things you do that are good for your teeth?

Are there things that are bad for your teeth?

How does brushing your teeth help?

Questions

What do you think about our ideas now?

Are there any more questions to answer?

✳ What kind of teeth do you have? Are they all the same type?

✳ Why do you think that teeth are different shapes? What do the different kinds of teeth do?

✳ Different animals eat different kinds of food. Can you think why?

✳ Do you think that all animals have the same kinds of teeth that we have? Why do you think that?

✳ What should you do to look after your teeth? What kinds of things might not be very good for your teeth? How does brushing them help?

✳ How do you know that your ideas are right?

✳ Why don't you make a chart to show what different animals eat and what kinds of teeth they have?

The big idea in this story is that animals need different teeth because they eat different foods.

There are different kinds of teeth. The main types are:

INCISOR TEETH
These are sharp and shaped like a chisel.

CANINE TEETH
These are long, sharp and pointed.

MOLAR TEETH
These are big, wide teeth.

The different types of teeth are used in different ways.

Incisor teeth are used for cutting and gnawing food. They're a bit like scissors.

Canine teeth are used for stabbing and tearing food.

Molar teeth are used for grinding and chewing food.

Different animals eat different foods. They need the right kind of teeth to eat their food.

Sheep and rabbits are

HERBIVORES

• Herbivores have special incisor teeth to gnaw and nibble plants and flat molars to grind the plants.

• Carnivores have fanglike canine teeth for stabbing and ripping meat. Their molars are sharp edged to help to chew flesh and bone.

Crocodiles and tigers are

CARNIVORES

Brilliant Beans

Nana and Ricky arrived at the park entrance. The day of the Autumn Fair had arrived at last. They were keen to see who had grown the best fruit and vegetables. They knew that Ruby and Jed had some vegetables in the show and might even win a prize!

They stopped at one table. It was filled with big, round apples. "These are amazing apples," Ricky said.

They stopped at another table. It was filled with long, fat beans. "These are brilliant beans," Nana said.

A third table was filled with plump, juicy tomatoes. "These are terrific tomatoes," Ricky said. It was a very impressive show this year.

Jed was standing near the next table. It was filled with carrots. Nana picked one up. "This will never win a prize," she thought when she looked at the carrot. "Look at this! It's the worst carrot in the show."

"It's mine," said Jed, looking sad.

Ruby was standing near the next table. It was filled with onions. Ricky picked one up. "This will never win a prize," he thought when he looked at the onion. "Look at this! It's the worst onion in the show."

"It's mine," said Ruby, looking sad. "Nothing seemed to grow well this year," Ruby explained. "All our vegetables are hopeless. Perhaps I should ask Little Wizard to do a spell for us so that they grow better next time."

Little Wizard was at the cake competition. He was busily waving his wand around. Grandad had asked him for a spell to make his fairy cakes rise. But floating cakes wasn't quite what he had in mind!

"I'm not sure if Little Wizard can help you," Ricky replied. "Maybe you haven't grown them properly. Perhaps you left something out that helps them to grow."

So Ruby, Ricky, Nana and Jed started to talk about what they needed to do to win a prize next year. They all had different ideas.

Try to think of your own ideas for finding out.
Here are some of our ideas for what you could do...

Why not grow some vegetables? What helps them to grow well? You need some young healthy plants, such as beans, peas or cress.

Try growing them:

- ◎ with different amounts of light

- ◎ with different amounts of water

- ◎ in different temperatures.

How can you keep your test fair?

What else might make a difference?

- ◎ What if you cut off leaves or roots?

- ◎ What if you give your plants compost?

You could make a vegetable plot. See who can grow the biggest vegetables.

Ask a gardener for handy hints. Is there a vegetable show near you?

Why not keep a photo-diary of your investigations?

Use books or the internet to find out how to grow vegetables.

Questions

What do you think about our ideas now?

Are there any more questions to answer?

* What do you think might have happened to Ruby and Jed's vegetables?

* Do all vegetables need the same things to grow well?

* Why do you think plants have roots and leaves?

* How do gardeners help their plants to grow well?

* What would you do to try to grow the biggest vegetables?

* Where do you think the vegetables in the shops come from? Why do some come from different countries?

* How do you know that your ideas are right?

* Why not make a gardeners' guide to growing the best vegetables? You could include photos or make a video.

The big idea in this story is that plants need different things if they are to grow properly.

Plants normally only grow well if they have the right conditions.
Most plants need:

★ plenty of light

★ quite a lot of water

★ good soil or compost

★ to be warm.

Some plants can grow in unusual conditions.

Ferns will grow in shady places.

A **cactus** can grow without much water.

Peas grow well in cool temperatures.

Air plants don't need soil.

Leaves use the sunlight to help the plants grow.

Gardeners sometimes give their plants extra help.
They might grow them in a greenhouse; water them when they are dry; give them special soil or compost or make sure they do not get too cold.

Roots anchor the plant and take water and minerals from the soil.

Frank's Fabulous Fish and Chips

A new fish and chip shop had opened in town. Nana and Ricky looked at the sign outside. 'Frank's Fabulous Fish and Chips, EVERYONE GETS A PRESENT!' It had started to rain but they didn't mind. They'd never had a present in a fish and chip shop before. "Shall we go in?" asked Ricky eagerly. But Nana was already heading through the door. She loved surprises.

They were excited as they stood in the queue. Now it was their turn. Frank made two piles of tasty fish and chips. Then he wrapped them carefully in beautiful wrapping paper and left the two brightly coloured parcels on the counter in front of them. They really did look just like presents!

They stood outside the shop under the sign for Frank's Fabulous Fish and Chips. Although it was still raining, they couldn't wait to get into their parcels.

Nana's parcel started to get wet in the rain. "This is no good Ricky," she said. "Look, the colour from the wrapping paper is running onto my chips! And the paper is beginning to fall apart where it's wet!"

Ricky didn't reply. As he started to unwrap his parcel, the paper tore and several chips fell onto the floor. "Oh no, I'm losing my chips!" he shouted. Nana and Ricky went straight back into the shop with their parcels.

Nana showed Frank how the colour had run onto her chips. "This wrapping paper isn't any good," she said. "My chips are ruined."

Ricky showed Frank where the paper had torn and his chips had fallen out. "This wrapping paper isn't any good," he said. "My chips are ruined."

Frank looked sad. He agreed to give Nana and Ricky some extra chips to replace the ones that had been ruined. "Perhaps you can help me," he said. "My customers like getting their fish and chips in lovely wrapping paper, but some of it isn't very good. I don't know which kind of wrapping paper is best to use."

Just then Ruby and Jed arrived. They had come to buy some fish and chips too. They started to talk about what kind of wrapping paper to use. They all had different ideas about which kind of paper would be best.

Try to think of your own ideas for finding out. Here are some of our ideas for what you could do...

Why not explore different types of wrapping paper? You could make parcels with them.

Which paper do you think Frank should use in his shop?

How are fish and chips normally wrapped?

See if you can find out why fish and chips are put in newspaper, layers of white paper, boxes or polystyrene trays.

Why do you think that there are so many different types of paper?

Can you match the different papers to how they are used?

You could investigate lots of different types of wrapping paper to see which might be best.

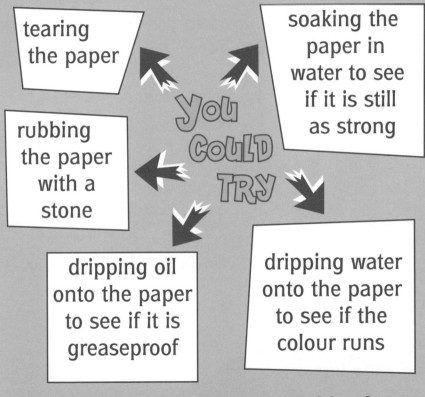

tearing the paper

soaking the paper in water to see if it is still as strong

rubbing the paper with a stone

YOU COULD TRY

dripping oil onto the paper to see if it is greaseproof

dripping water onto the paper to see if the colour runs

Are there any other tests you could try? How will you make your tests fair?

Questions

What do you think about our ideas now?

Are there any more questions to answer?

✳ Which is the best paper for Frank to use? Why would you tell him to use this paper?

✳ How did you find out your answer? Can you think of other ways to find out?

✳ Why do we have so many different kinds of paper? What different jobs do they do?

✳ Which would be the best paper for wiping a runny nose?

✳ Which would be the best paper for making a disposable coffee cup?

✳ How do you know that your ideas are right?

✳ Why not make a chart for Frank to help him decide which wrapping paper is best for making his parcels of chips?

FRANK'S FABULOUS FISH & CHIPS

The big idea in this story is that different materials have different properties. This makes them suitable for some uses but not for others.

Different materials are used for different purposes.

★ Wood and iron are very strong, so they're used for cars and furniture.

★ Rubber is very stretchy, so it's used for elastic bands.

★ Glass is transparent, so it's used for windows and jam jars.

★ Gold and silver are shiny and can bend, so they're used for jewellery.

Paper, like other materials, can be used in different ways.

★ Paper towel absorbs water, so it's good for mopping up spills.

★ Crepe paper is colourful and textured, so it's useful for decorations.

★ Writing paper is smooth and not very absorbent, so it's good for writing on.

★ Tissue paper is soft, so it's good for protecting delicate objects.

Several layers of plain white paper are often used for wrapping chips. It's cheap, quite strong, doesn't have runny colours and helps to keep the fish and chips warm. But it doesn't look very exciting.

BIG New Book of Spells

Disappearing Soil

Every year Nana and Ricky grow fantastic flowers. The soil in Nana's garden is deep and dark and rich. It's perfect for growing things. Today Nana and Ricky are excited. They've bought some new plants from the market and are looking forward to putting them in the flowerbed.

They went to the shed to collect some tools. Nana took a spade and put it carefully in the wheelbarrow. Ricky chose a fork and put it neatly next to the spade. Then they wheeled the wheelbarrow down the garden.

Suddenly, there was a whooshing sound and Little Wizard appeared on the bench in front of them. He was frantically reading the pages of his Big New Book of Spells, muttering to himself and looking very anxious indeed. Nana and Ricky wondered what was wrong with Little Wizard. Then they looked at the flowerbed. They could both see instantly what the problem was.

"Where has all the soil gone?" Nana gasped. "Have you been practising your spells again?" It didn't look anything like her flowerbed. There wasn't any soil to be seen anywhere, just lots of little stones and some very droopy flowers.

"Let me try another one," Little Wizard mumbled, waving his wand and reading aloud from his book of spells. "Bibble, babble, bobble, bones, take away these broken stones."

Suddenly the little stones started to shake. "Stop it, Little Wizard, you're making it even worse!" Ricky shouted. Now all they could see was rocks and boulders where the soil used to be.

"Oh dear," Little Wizard sighed, "What have I done? I just wanted to help your flowers to grow. I'm sure that I must have a spell to get the soil back again. If only I knew what soil was made from."

Then Ruby and Jed came down the path. They enjoyed spending time in Nana's garden. Ricky explained why the soil had disappeared and why they needed to work out how soil is made. No one had thought about soil before, so they all had different ideas.

Try to think of your own ideas for finding out.
Here are some of our ideas for what you could do...

CHECK WITH AN ADULT

Find out what soil looks like.

Dig a deep hole or look at a hole that has already been dug. Is the soil the same everywhere in the hole?

Find out what's underneath the soil if you could dig a long way down.

Wear gloves to handle soil and wash your hands afterwards.

Are there any animals in soil?

Think about what they might do to help to make soil.

Try making a wormery and observe what worms do.

Set up a compost heap.

COMPOST HEAPS USE GARDEN AND KITCHEN WASTE

Find out what is in soil. You could:

⊚ look at it using a hand lens or microscope

⊚ put it through a sieve to separate the bits

⊚ shake it with water and see what happens

⊚ look in books and on the internet.

Find out whether all soil is the same.

You could look at soil from a. . .

› SANDY AREA (like a seaside town)
› PEATY AREA (like a moorland)
› CHALKY AREA and a CLAY AREA.

Questions

What do you think about our ideas now?

Are there any more questions to answer?

✳ Why do you think that soil has bits of rock in it? Where could they have come from?

✳ Worms help to make compost and soil. How do they do it?

✳ Do you think that other animals help to make soil? How?

✳ Is there anything else we might find in soil if we look carefully?

✳ Is soil the same everywhere? Why might it be different in different places?

✳ Where do you think that the soil in garden centres comes from?

✳ How do you know that your ideas are right?

✳ Why don't you try to write a recipe for soil so that Little Wizard can do a better spell?

PEAT FREE COMPOST

The big idea in this story is that different things go together to make soil.

Soil is made up of different things. You can see the different bits by using a magnifier or microscope.

Usually soil contains:

★ tiny pieces of crushed-up rock

★ bits of dead plants and animals

★ air

★ water.

The different parts of the soil are used in different ways.

★ Plants need the water to help them to grow.

★ Worms and other animals need the air to breathe. They help to break down dead plants and animals.

★ Dead bits of plants and animals rot, and this recycles minerals into the soil. Plants need the minerals to help them to grow.

Soil is different in different places because the rocks that make the soil are different.

Soil is created when all the different bits come together in the same place. Water helps to hold the different bits of soil together. This happens naturally. Soil does not need to be made by people.

The animals, plants and climate can make a difference too.

Maggie from Magnetti

It was the start of Foreign Exchange Week. Visitors from different places were coming to the school. Ruby and Ricky were excited. They had been asked to look after one of them. She was called Maggie. There was a small group of visitors waiting nervously on the playground. They wondered which one she would be. Then Nana spotted one of the visitors floating towards them.

"Hi, Ruby. Hi, Ricky. My name is Maggie." Maggie waved two arms at Ruby and Ricky. "I'm from planet Magnetti," she continued, pointing up into the sky. "I've been wanting to come to Earth for ages."

"Wow! I've never met anybody from planet Magnetti before. What's it like there?" Ruby was bursting with excitement.

Maggie just smiled. "I'll tell you later," she said, "but I need some help first. I seem to be rather sticky. Look!" Maggie waggled one of her arms. There was a wire coat hanger sticking to it!

"Sticky? What do you mean?" asked Ricky. Maggie didn't answer. Instead she went inside the classroom. She put one of her hands near a pair of scissors. The scissors stuck to her hand! When she went near the door, it slowly opened as the handle stuck to her hand!

Then she put one of her fingers in the paper clip tray. Her finger came out covered in paper clips! "I think I know what the problem is," Ruby said. "You're magnetic!"

"Yes, let me show you," Ricky added. He put a magnet into the paper clip tray. It came out covered in paper clips, just like Maggie's finger.

"I think we can help you, Maggie," Ruby continued. "You just need to avoid things that might stick to a magnet."

Maggie floated out of the classroom. She sat on the wall in the playground near Jed and Nana. Her eyes blinked, her arms waved and she made some very strange noises. They could see that Maggie was very confused.

All they needed to do was decide what would be magnetic and then Maggie would be happy again. The trouble was they all had different ideas.

Try to think of your own ideas for finding out.
Here are some of our ideas for what you could do...

You could have fun exploring what will stick to Maggie.

Try things such as:

pens, coins, paper,
coat hangers, paper clips,
badges, rings, drinks cans, nails,
drawing pins, etc.

Use books or the internet to find out what **MAGNETIC** means and where magnets are used.

Go on an expedition to find hidden magnets.

Explore magnets:

- Can you make them pull or push things?
- How far away do they work?
- Do they work through things?
- How strong are they?
- Are they all the same?

Do you need to carry out a fair test to answer some of these questions?

Make up a 'Maggie from Magnetti' game using magnets. How will you play it?

Questions

What do you think about our ideas now?

Are there any more questions to answer?

✳ Why do you think that Maggie is sticky?

✳ What will stick to Maggie? What won't stick to Maggie?

✳ Somebody said that all metals stick to magnets. Are they right?

✳ Are all magnets the same? Are some stronger than others?

✳ Somebody said that if something is MAGNETIC it has a magnet inside it. What do you think?

✳ Where are magnets used? What are they used for?

✳ How do you know that your ideas are right?

✳ Why don't you finish the story about Maggie's visit? You can draw pictures to show what happens to her.

The big idea in this story is that some materials are attracted to magnets. We call them magnetic materials.

Not many materials are attracted to magnets.

★ Iron, and steel (which is made from iron), are magnetic.

★ Objects that have some iron in them, like door handles and paperclips, will stick to a magnet.

★ Objects with magnetic material inside them might trick you into thinking plastic, wood and other materials are magnetic.

Magnets do interesting things.

★ They can stick to each other and can push each other away.

★ They have different strengths.

★ They can work through things. A magnet under the table could move a paperclip on top.

Nickel, cobalt and magnetite rocks are also magnetic.

Magnets are used:

• to make compasses (a compass is really a tiny magnet)

• to keep fridge doors closed • to fasten bags

• in some toys • inside electric motors.

Magnetic materials can be made into magnets.

Dear Ruby and Ricky,
I'm locked in the big tower.
There are guards at the door and
guards at the bottom of the tower.
I only have one window. I've been locked
in for three years. Please help me.
from The Princess

The Prisoner Princess

Ruby and Ricky were waiting for the mail to arrive. They always liked getting letters and postcards from interesting places.

Today there was a mysterious looking letter. It was addressed to Ruby and Ricky.

They opened the letter carefully. Inside was a single piece of paper. It read, . . . Dear Ruby and Ricky . . . .

Ruby and Ricky wanted to help the princess. So they hurried over to the big tower. It was enormous! They could hardly see to the top.

Ruby looked at Ricky. Ricky looked at Ruby. They both looked at the tower. It was so big. How could they possibly help the princess to escape?

Ricky suggested that they could bring a ladder to rescue the princess during the night. She could use the ladder to climb down from the window when the guards left.

"That's a good idea Ricky," said Ruby, "but how will we know how big the ladder needs to be? We don't want to come back during the night and find that the ladder is too short!"

They both looked at the guards at the bottom of the tower. They looked very fierce, with helmets and swords. They could see the shadow of the tower on the ground. The shadow was VERY big.

"I'll tell you what, Ricky," Ruby continued, "we could measure the shadow of the tower. Then we will know how big the tower is." Ruby was pleased that they had thought of a way to rescue the princess.

Ricky looked uncertain. He wasn't sure that the shadow would be the same size as the tower.

Just then Nana and Jed arrived. Ruby and Ricky had told them about the princess trapped in the tower. Ruby explained that they needed to measure the height of the tower so they could help her to escape. They all thought about whether measuring the shadow would help, then they started to talk about their ideas.

The Prisoner Princess © Brenda Keogh and Stuart Naylor 2007

Try to think of your own ideas for finding out.
Here are some of our ideas for what you could do...

CHECK WITH AN ADULT

Make a model tower out of cardboard, wood or bricks outside on a sunny day.

Draw round the shadow ...

◉ in the morning

◉ at lunchtime

◉ just before you go home.

What do you notice? You could try doing this once a month. Do you see any differences?

DON'T stare at the Sun.

You could make a model of a tower out of card and use a torch for the Sun.

◉ How long is the shadow if you shine the torch on the tower?

◉ How can you change the shadow?

◉ Is the shadow ever the same size as the tower?

You could use books or the internet to find out more about shadows. Sundials use shadows. You could find out about them too.

Measure your shadow at different times on a sunny day. Is it always the same size?

Can you change the size?

Is it always in the same place?

Look for photographs of objects and their shadows. Are the shadows longer or shorter than the object?

Questions

What do you think about our ideas now?

Are there any more questions to answer?

✳ Do you think all our different ideas can be right?

✳ Would measuring the shadow help the princess?

✳ What do you think makes a difference to the length of a shadow?

✳ Sundials use shadows. Do you know how they work?

✳ Why don't we get shadows at night?

✳ Can you think of any other ways to find out how big the tower is?

✳ How do you know that your ideas are right?

✳ Why don't you finish the story to show what happened when the shadow was measured and how the princess was rescued?

The big idea in this story is that the position of the Sun in the sky changes during the day. The size and direction of shadows caused by the Sun also change.

When something blocks the light you get a shadow.

★ The Sun can make a shadow.

★ A torch or a lamp can make a shadow.

★ The shadow is on the opposite side of the object from the light.

As the Earth rotates, the Sun appears to move across the sky and the length of shadows changes.

★ The Sun is low in the sky in the morning and evening. When the Sun is low shadows are long.

★ The Sun is highest in the sky at midday. When the Sun is high in the sky, shadows are short.

But they could find the length of the shadow of a metre stick.

The length of the tower's shadow changes during the day. This makes it tricky for Ricky and Ruby to use the shadow to find the height of the tower.

Then they could find how many times the metre stick's shadow fits into the tower's shadow.

A Bony Problem

Nana pointed at the plaster cast on Ricky's arm. "How does it feel, Ricky? Does it still hurt a lot?"

Nana, Ricky and Ruby were at the hospital. Ricky had fallen out of a tree and broken his arm. He had been taken to the hospital in an ambulance.

"It's OK now," Ricky replied. "It hurt a lot more when I hit the ground."

Ricky lifted his arm up to see how heavy the plaster cast was. It wasn't too bad. He couldn't wait to show all his friends. He might even let them draw on it.

When Nana and Ricky got back from the hospital, they went to the park. Nana wanted to see where Ricky had been climbing when he fell.

They had only walked a short distance when Ricky stopped and pointed to an oak tree. "Look Nana, it's this one. I was sitting on that branch when I fell off."

Nana opened her mouth and then closed it again. She was going to tell Ricky to be more careful in future, but she decided there was no point. He probably wouldn't take any notice. Instead she carefully knelt down next to something in the grass. "What's that Nana?" asked Ricky. "Let me see what's in your hand."

Nana held out her hand. She was holding a worm. "These worms are sensible," she said. "They stay on the ground so they don't fall and break their bones."

"They can't break their bones, Nana. I don't think that they have any bones!" Ricky replied, as he gently touched the worm. "I wish I was like a worm. If I didn't have any bones then I wouldn't be able to break them when I fall. Perhaps I'll see if Little Wizard can do a spell to get rid of them."

Nana thought that was an odd idea, but she didn't say anything.

Just then Jed and Ruby arrived. They heard Ricky talking about being like a worm. It sounded like a really interesting idea. So they all began to talk about what would happen if he didn't have any bones.

Try to think of your own ideas for finding out.
Here are some of our ideas for what you could do...

Try drawing the skeleton of a:

- ⊚ Fish
- ⊚ Worm
- ⊚ Snake
- ⊚ Human
- ⊚ Snail
- ⊚ Crab
- ⊚ Cat
- ⊚ Fly
- ⊚ Bird
- ⊚ Giraffe

Were your drawings right?

You can explore bones and skeletons of different animals:

- ⊚ in a museum or other collection
- ⊚ in books or CDs
- ⊚ on the internet
- ⊚ in a web image search for 'skeletons'.

Think about:

- ⊚ which bits of your body might get damaged easily
- ⊚ if a skeleton protects any of these bits.

Find out how bones and muscles help you to move.

Watch each other moving.

Feel your own bones and muscles.

Bones are usually hollow tubes. Make hollow tubes out of paper and explore how strong they are.

Questions

* What kinds of animals have bones?

* Why do you think we have bones? What do you think would happen if we didn't have any bones?

* How do you think worms avoid getting damaged? How do other animals manage without any bones?

* If bones are hollow tubes why don't they break when we jump up and down?

* Why do you think bones break? Why does putting your arm in plaster help to fix it?

* How do you know that your ideas are right?

* Why not write a story about what it would be like if you didn't have any bones?

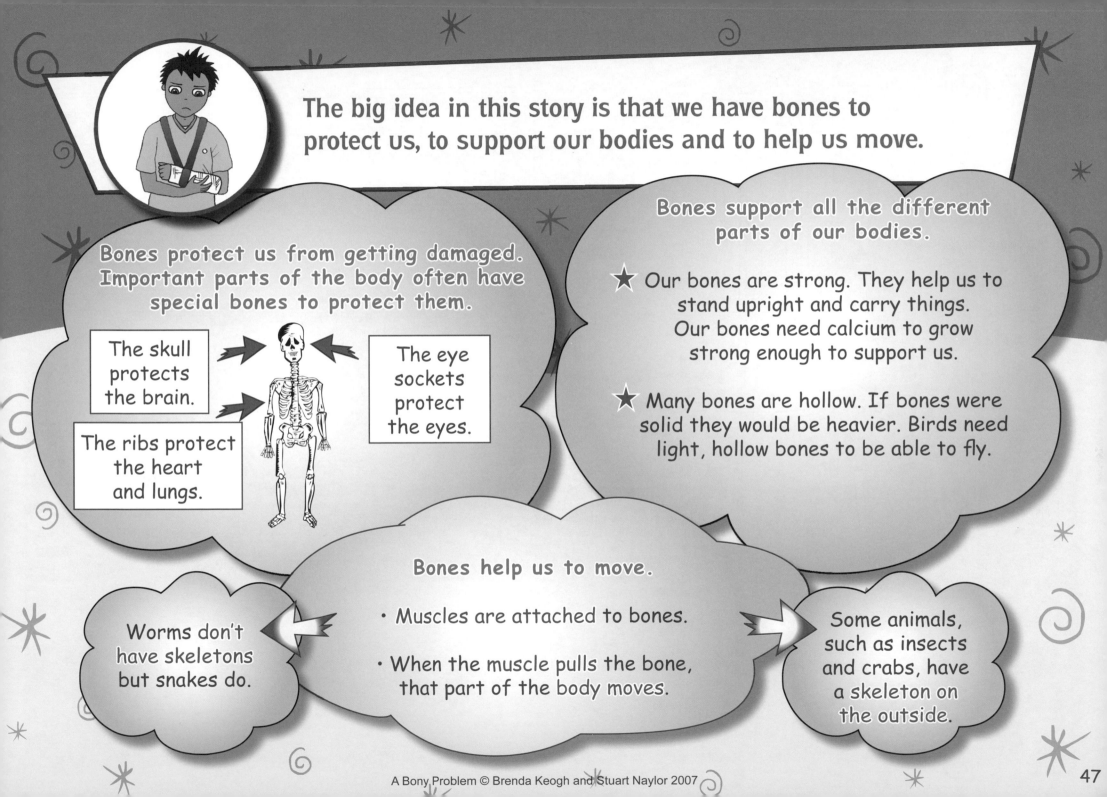

The big idea in this story is that we have bones to protect us, to support our bodies and to help us move.

Bones protect us from getting damaged. Important parts of the body often have special bones to protect them.

The skull protects the brain.

The ribs protect the heart and lungs.

The eye sockets protect the eyes.

Bones support all the different parts of our bodies.

★ Our bones are strong. They help us to stand upright and carry things. Our bones need calcium to grow strong enough to support us.

★ Many bones are hollow. If bones were solid they would be heavier. Birds need light, hollow bones to be able to fly.

Bones help us to move.

• Muscles are attached to bones.

• When the muscle pulls the bone, that part of the body moves.

Worms don't have skeletons but snakes do.

Some animals, such as insects and crabs, have a skeleton on the outside.

A Hoppy Home

Plip, plip, plip, . . . plip, plip. Ricky looked puzzled. "What's that sound, Nana?" he asked. "I keep hearing it."

"It's the young frogs," Nana replied. "I've seen them hopping about a lot recently. You'll see them too, if you look carefully." And when Nana and Ricky looked down they could see a line of young frogs, slowly hopping away from the pond.

Plip, plip, as they hopped onto the grass by the pond. Plip, . . plip, plip, as they hopped across the path.

"I wonder why they're all leaving the pond," said Ricky. "It's hot today. Wouldn't they be better staying in the pond?" Nana replied, "Now that the tadpoles have turned into frogs, it's too crowded for them all to live in the pond. They are leaving to find a new home."

One of the frogs heard what Nana and Ricky were saying. It stopped hopping. "This pond is our home," it said. "But we have to leave now. We're homeless." Another frog hopped over to them. "How will we find another home?" it asked. "We don't know where to live now."

Nana and Ricky watched the line of young frogs hopping away across the garden. They wondered how they could help them to find a new place to live.

The last young frog jumped off a lily pad and hopped quickly down the path to join them. "We need to advertise for a new home," it shouted when it had almost caught up with them. "Perhaps we could put an advert in the Frog Gazette. Will you help us to produce an advert?" And the frog held out a copy of the Frog Gazette to show Nana and Ricky.

"An advert in the Frog Gazette!" Ricky exclaimed. "I'm sure we can do something." So Nana and Ricky thought about what kind of advert they would need. It wasn't easy. Where was the best place for frogs to live? Every idea that they came up with just didn't seem right.

They followed the frogs out of the garden. Jed and Ruby had arrived and were waiting to go swimming with Ricky. They were fascinated watching the young frogs. Nana explained the problem to them. They thought hard about what they should say in the advert and then all started to talk about their ideas.

Try to think of your own ideas for finding out. Here are some of our ideas for what you could do...

CHECK WITH AN ADULT

You can use books, CDs or the internet to find out more about the places where frogs like to live.

- ☺ What do frogs eat?
- ☺ What eats frogs?
- ☺ How do frogs keep safe?
- ☺ Why is it hard to spot them?
- ☺ Do all types of frogs live in the same kinds of places?

Talk to an adult if you are thinking of going near ponds.

Perhaps you could go outside to look for where frogs are living. Take care not to disturb them.

- ☺ Where do you see them?
- ☺ Are they only in the water?
- ☺ Listen carefully, you might hear them calling.

You could write to a wildlife expert or visit a field centre to find out what experts think.

Find out about the life cycle of a frog.

When is the best time to see tadpoles or froglets?

Find out more about FROGWATCH and other wildlife protection schemes.

Questions

✳ Have you seen frogs in real life? Where have you seen them?

✳ Where will be good places for the frogs to live?   Why do you think that?

✳ Do frogs need to be in water all the time?

✳ Would there be a problem if none of the frogs left the pond?

✳ What else do you think might live in the pond? Will they have to leave as well?

✳ How do you know that your ideas are right?

✳ Why don't you make an advert for the Frog Gazette to advertise for a new home for the frogs?

The big idea in this story is that animals and plants are suited to the places where they live.

Frogs are suited to living on land in damp, shady places and in water. They don't live in water all the time. They are amphibians.

★ They breathe through their moist skin.

★ They eat things that live in damp places, such as worms and insects.

★ They lay their eggs in water.

★ They can swim well in water and jump well on land.

Other animals and plants are suited to living in different places.

 Polar bears have white fur. They are camouflaged against the snow.

Fish have fins and gills. They can swim and breathe well in water.

Pondweed and seaweed can live in water, even though most plants can't.

If too many of one type of animal or plant stay in one place they will compete with each other and may run out of food and die. As animals grow into adults they tend to move to other suitable habitats. Plants also have ways of spreading out (dispersing).

The Ice Bird

It was a cold, crisp night. There was a big moon in the sky, the windows were frosted and the grass sparkled on the ground. Little Wizard was standing in the garden with Ricky and Ruby.

He waved his wand about as he spoke. "This is exactly the kind of night when the ice bird comes. I can feel the magic in my wand. If only you could see it. Its ice feathers shimmer in the moonlight and, if you listen carefully, you can hear the tinkling of its icicle toes."

Ruby pulled her hat on tighter. She looked doubtful. She had never seen an ice bird. Why would one come to their garden? "You always get in a muddle Little Wizard. I'm going in," she said. "It's freezing out here."

"Just wait till the morning. You'll see!" said Little Wizard. "If the ice bird has been it's because it has chosen you to look after its ice eggs. But you need to be careful or they will melt and I don't know the spell to stop them."

Before they could ask him a single question, Little Wizard waved his wand and disappeared into the night.

The next day was bright and sunny. Ricky and Ruby rushed out into the garden. Was Little Wizard right for once? Had they missed the ice bird? Would they find any eggs?

And then they saw them. Ice bird eggs! Partly hidden near the big tree. There were six of them. They were big, the biggest eggs Ricky and Ruby had ever seen.

Ricky stretched out to touch them. They were very cold. They were made of ice just like Little Wizard had said.

"Ricky," Ruby whispered anxiously, "what if the eggs melt when you touch them?"

Ricky got his mobile out to phone Nana and Jed. "The ice bird! It's been! It's laid some eggs! Come round and look!"

So Nana and Jed rushed round. They could hardly believe it. Ice bird eggs glistening in the sun. But they could also see tiny droplets of water. The eggs were beginning to melt! What should they do? They had to think of a good way to stop the eggs melting but they all had different ideas.

Try to think of your own ideas for finding out.
Here are some of our ideas for what you could do...

You can make your own ice bird eggs.

1. Get some balloons.
2. Fill them with water by putting them over the end of the tap.
3. Place them in a bowl.
4. Then leave them in the freezer for a few days.

Can you find out how cold it needs to be to keep the eggs?

Use a thermometer to find out which places are warm and which are cold.

Find out more about what animals do to keep themselves warm or cool.

What if the eggs have to stay outside so that the ice bird can find them?

How could you keep them cold?

You could put your ICE eggs (or ice cubes) in different materials.

You could try:

- Wool
- Cold water
- Foil
- Bubblewrap
- Cling film
- Newspaper
- Black bin liner
- Polystyrene chips

What else can you try? How can you make sure that your test is fair?

Questions

* Why do you think the ice bird lays its eggs at night?

* What might happen to the ice bird's eggs in the daytime? Why?

* What might happen if we touch the ice bird's eggs? Why?

* Which materials should we use to wrap the ice bird's eggs? Why do you think that is the best?

* Someone said that materials that stop the eggs melting are called insulators. What does that mean?

* What other things can we use insulators for?

* How do you know your ideas are right?

* Why don't you paint or draw a picture of the ice bird returning to check that the eggs haven't melted?

The big idea in this story is that some materials do not let heat pass through them easily. They are called insulators. They help to keep things cold.

Things with lots of air spaces in them are good insulators. Heat does not pass through air very easily.

★ Wool has lots of air spaces.

★ Bubble wrap has lots of air spaces.

★ Foam has lots of air spaces.

Ricky and Ruby could use one of these to stop the ice eggs from melting.

Some materials are good at passing on heat. We call these conductors.

★ Many metals are good conductors, for example aluminium foil.

★ Ricky and Ruby shouldn't use foil to protect the eggs from the warmth of the sun. The heat will pass through the foil and melt the eggs.

Putting the eggs in cold water wouldn't help.

• Even though the water is very cold, it will still be warmer than the eggs.

• The eggs will be surrounded by the water and will normally melt even faster than if they were left in the air.

We use an insulator to keep things hot or cold. Cool boxes and thermos flasks are good insulators.

An insulator will keep hot things hot and keep cold things cold.

Picnic on the Beach © Brenda Keogh and Stuart Naylor 2007

Picnic on the Beach

"Have a look at this Nana." Ricky put his spade down. "I don't think I have ever built a sandcastle this big before."

Nana took a few steps back to get a good view. It certainly was big. It had four deep layers, four round turrets and a wide moat. "It's fantastic, Ricky! And look, you finished it just in time."

As they watched, the sea started to pour into the moat. Soon the moat was full. The waves washed round the bottom of the sandcastle and the first turret started to crumble. In a little while the sandcastle would be gone.

Nana and Ricky walked back up the beach away from the sea. It had been a wonderful morning. They had paddled in the water, flown Ricky's new red kite and ridden on a donkey. Now it was time for their picnic.

Nana unwrapped the food and put it out on the blanket. They had sandwiches, fruit, chocolate and drinks.

Ricky poured Nana a cup of tea and added some sugar. She liked a bit of sugar in her tea. "Won't be long now Nana. I think the sugar has nearly melted," he said.

"Melted?" Nana replied. "I thought sugar dissolved."

Ricky was busy unwrapping a bar of chocolate. It had been in the sun for a while. It was very soft and squishy. "Ugh! How are we going to eat this? It's beginning to melt."

"Melt?" Nana replied. " Doesn't chocolate dissolve?"

Ricky didn't reply. He needed a drink. So he poured some orange juice, took four ice cubes and dropped them in the glass. "Look at the ice Nana! Do you think it's dissolving or melting?"

"I'm not sure." Nana replied, "I think ice dissolves, but maybe it melts."

Just then Ruby and Jed came over to return Ricky's kite. Ricky explained that they were getting very confused about melting and dissolving. He pointed to where he had built his sandcastle, but it had almost disappeared. Had that melted too? Ruby and Jed weren't sure either. They all started to talk about their ideas.

Try to think of your own ideas for finding out.
Here are some of our ideas for what you could do...

CHECK WITH AN ADULT

Find out what happens when you leave things in the sun or on a radiator.

You could try:

- Sand
- Butter
- Coffee
- Jelly
- Wax
- Tea
- Ice cream
- Syrup
- Sugar
- Salt
- Chocolate
- Ice

Can you think of anything else to try?

DO NOT heat things without an adult's help.

Does the temperature make a difference to how quickly something melts?

Explore what happens next when the same things are put in the freezer.

Go on a 'Things That Melt' hunt.

What do you find?

Find out what happens when you mix the same things with water or other liquids.

Does the temperature make a difference to how quickly something dissolves?

Can you get them back again?

Go on a 'Things That Dissolve' hunt. What do you find?

Use the internet or a book to find out what MELT and DISSOLVE mean.

Questions

What do you think about our ideas now?

Are there any more questions to answer?

✳ Which things were melting? How do you know?

✳ Which things were dissolving? How do you know?

✳ What's the difference between melting and dissolving?

✳ If something melts how can you get it to turn back into a solid again?

✳ If something dissolves how can you get it back again?

✳ What do you think happened to the sandcastle?

✳ How do you know that your ideas are right?

✳ Why don't you write an information card to help us to decide which things melt, which things dissolve and which things don't seem to do either?

The big idea in this story is that melting and dissolving are different. They happen for different reasons.

Melting is when a solid turns into a liquid as it gets warmer.

★ Chocolate, ice and butter all melt when they get warm.

★ When they get colder they turn back into a solid (freeze).

★ Different materials melt and freeze at different temperatures. Water freezes at 0°C. Iron melts at 1535°C.

Dissolving is when a solid seems to disappear when it is mixed with a liquid.

★ The solid breaks up into bits that are so tiny that we can't see them. The bits are still there in the water.

★ It is possible to get them back again if the liquid evaporates.

★ Salt and sugar dissolve in water.

Some things, like wood, don't melt. When it gets hot, it burns and turns into carbon dioxide.

The sandcastle hasn't melted or dissolved. It has collapsed and the grains of sand have been swept away by the sea.

•Sand does not dissolve in any liquids at normal temperatures.
•Sand can melt at very high temperatures. This is used to make glass.

Some things like sugar and jelly can melt and dissolve.

An Irritating Day © Brenda Keogh and Stuart Naylor 2007

An Irritating Day

Nana and Ricky were getting ready to leave for school. It was a lovely sunny day – not too hot, a little bit of cloud and a gentle breeze. It was the kind of day that usually makes everybody feel good.

But today was different. Today everything seemed to be just a little bit odd. Today everybody seemed to be irritated.

Nana was irritated. She was making a cup of tea. When she picked up the cup it slipped out of her hand and broke on the floor. "Why did that happen?" she wondered.

Ricky was irritated. Something had gone wrong with his shoes. They didn't seem to be very grippy any more, so he kept falling over. "Why did that happen?" he wondered.

At the school it was obvious that something wasn't right. They saw a pigeon try to land on the roof but it just slid off. "Why did that happen?" asked Ricky.

They saw a postman, delivering letters, trying to stop on his bike. He went sailing straight past them. "Why did that happen?" asked Nana.

Little Wizard was waiting at the school door. Even he looked irritated! "I thought you two were never coming. I need your help, right now! I was practising spells and one of them went wrong, but I can't remember which spell it was. I don't know how to fix it."

Little Wizard tried to wave his wand but it slipped out of his hand and fell onto the floor. "It's been doing this all morning," sighed Little Wizard.

He picked up the wand again and started to wave it around furiously, hoping that might help. But it didn't make any difference. The wand simply flew out of his hand, did a somersault in the air and landed back on the ground.

Ruby and Jed arrived at school. They overheard Little Wizard talking about the problems he was having with his spells. Was this why everything seemed a little odd this morning and why they were feeling irritated too? They all started to talk about what might have gone wrong but they all had different ideas.

Try to think of your own ideas for finding out.
Here are some of our ideas for what you could do...

Find out about AIR RESISTANCE. You could explore things falling, such as pieces of paper, feathers, balloons. Which fall quickly and which fall slowly? Can you change the way that they fall?

TAKE CARE when dropping things.

Use books or the internet to find out about GRAVITY, AIR RESISTANCE and FRICTION.

Find out about FRICTION. You could investigate things sliding, such as shoes or blocks of wood. What makes them slide more quickly and what slows them down?

Think about why you are more likely to fall over on an icy day.

What's the different between:

◎ gravity ◎ air resistance

◎ and friction?

Can you find examples of the effects of gravity, air resistance and friction?

Find out about GRAVITY. Find out what it is like where gravity is less, like on the moon. Think about the way that things move and fall.

Imagine what life would be like if GRAVITY, AIR RESISTANCE or FRICTION increased or decreased.

Questions

✳ What do you think would happen if there is less gravity?

✳ What do you think would happen if there is more air resistance?

✳ What do you think would happen if friction is increased?

✳ What do you think would happen if friction is decreased?

✳ What do you think Little Wizard's spell has done?

✳ Can you make things less or more slippery without casting a spell?

✳ How do you know that your ideas are right?

✳ Why don't you draw some pictures or write a short story to show what would happen if Little Wizard's spell made friction increase?

What do you think about our ideas now?

Are there any more questions to answer?

The big idea in this story is that friction makes things grip. It stops them slipping and sliding.

Friction stops things slipping.
This is often very useful.
It helps us to:

★ pick things up (imagine your fingers coated in butter!)

★ walk (imagine walking on ice!)

★ ride a bike (imagine if tyres don't grip!).

If the spell increased friction, everything would be grippier.

Air resistance pushes against things that are moving.
We see this when:

★ a parachute falls slowly through the air

★ trees are blown over by the wind

★ we fly a kite.

If the spell increased air resistance things would move more slowly.

Gravity attracts things to the ground.

• When we drop a cup it falls because of gravity.

• When we throw a ball it falls because of gravity

If the spell reduced gravity things would be more floaty.

If the spell reduced friction everything would be slippier.

Little Wizard's spell must have reduced friction.

Curious Circuits

Ricky has a new bedroom. He's very excited to have a room of his own. Nana has been helping him to decorate it and now it's nearly finished. "Just this corner to paint," said Nana, "and then we'll all be done."

Ricky smiled. "There's one more thing," he said. "I need a doorbell so I'll know if someone wants to come in." He went to the cupboard where they had put all his toys. He opened the door. He could see the red box that they used to store the things for making circuits. He took the box down from the shelf.

"Oh no!" Ricky shouted, "I don't believe it!"

"What's wrong, what's happened?" Nana sounded worried. "Have you trapped your finger? Is the box full of spiders?"

Ricky held the box out for Nana to see. "Look! I can't believe what Little Wizard has done!"

Nana looked inside the box. She could see batteries, lamps, buzzers and other bits and pieces. But she couldn't see a single wire. Not one.

All she could see was a small note, in Little Wizard's handwriting. She picked up the note to read what it said.

Ricky groaned. "Well what's that supposed to mean? What other stuff is there? Everybody knows that you can't make circuits without any wires."

> I've had a problem with my new spell, and needed some wires to make it work well. I've borrowed your wires, so I'll have enough. You'll have to make circuits with some other stuff.
>
> L W

Nana looked thoughtful. "Hang on a minute, Ricky," she said. "Let's just think about this. Other things must conduct electricity as well as wires. Can we use something instead of wires to make a circuit?"

At that point Ruby and Jed turned up to see Ricky's new room. Nana explained that Little Wizard had taken all their wires but they wanted to make a doorbell. They all started to talk about whether they could make a circuit without any wires. They all had different ideas.

Try to think of your own ideas for finding out.
Here are some of our ideas for what you could do...

Try making a simple circuit using a buzzer, a battery and some wire.

Can you get the buzzer to work?

NEVER use mains electricity or rechargeable batteries.

You can set up a simple circuit to test materials. Put different things in your circuit to investigate what conducts electricity and what doesn't.

What do you find out?

BUZZER

Now explore what happens when you don't have any wires. Instead of wire you could try:

◎ String
◎ Aluminium foil
◎ A pencil
◎ A nail
◎ A plastic spoon
◎ A chain of paper clips

What else can you try?

Can you use books, the internet or talk to an expert to find out what other people think about what conducts electricity?

You could find out how things that **DO NOT** conduct electricity (insulators) help to keep us safe.

Questions

What do you think about our ideas now?

Are there any more questions to answer?

✳ How can we make the buzzer work with wires?

✳ How can we make the buzzer work without wires?

✳ Which things worked well? Which things didn't work?

✳ Someone said that things that help the buzzer to work are called conductors. Can you explain what that means?

✳ Someone said that things that don't help to make the buzzer work are called insulators. Can you explain what that means?

✳ How do insulators help to keep us safe?

✳ How do you know that your ideas are right?

✳ Why not write a poem or song to tell Little Wizard how you solved the problem?

The big idea in this story is that other things conduct electricity as well as wires.

Materials that allow electricity to flow easily are called conductors.

★ Metals, for example, copper, iron, silver, gold and aluminium, conduct electricity.

★ Some other things, such as carbon, conduct electricity. There are not many of these things.

★ Water conducts electricity. It is very dangerous to use electrical equipment near water or with wet hands.

Many things around us don't conduct electricity. We call them insulators.

★ Wood, glass, paper, plastic, string and rubber don't conduct electricity.

★ Some metal things, such as paper clips, can have a plastic coating. Electricity cannot flow through the plastic.

★ Plastic is used around wires to keep us safe.

To make the buzzer work, Ricky needs to make a circuit.

Thin bendy metal things will be the easiest to use.

It would be tricky to use a line of metal spoons.

A thin strip of aluminium foil would work well.

A line of paper clips will work too.